Our Country's Symbols

Sarah Machajewski

INFOMAX COMMON CORE READERS

Rosen Classroom™

New York

I0792472

Published in 2013 by The Rosen Publishing Group, Inc.
29 East 21st Street, New York, NY 10010

Book Design: Katelyn Londino

Photo Credits: Cover Patrick Rolands/Shutterstock.com; p. 4 VisionsofAmerica/Joe Sohm/Digital Vision/Getty Images; p. 5 gary718/Shutterstock.com; pp. 6, 22 (flag) Steve Collender/Shutterstock.com; pp. 7, 23 (flag) Brandon Jennings/Shutterstock.com; pp. 8, 22 (White House) Vacclav/Shutterstock.com; p. 9 Gary Blakeley/Shutterstock.com; pp. 10, 22, 23 (Washington Monument) Travel Bug/Shutterstock.com; p. 10 (Vietnam War Veteran Memorial) Jorg Hackemann/Shutterstock.com; p. 11 (World Trade Center Memorial) JustASC/Shutterstock.com; p. 11 (World War II Memorial) Joe Mercier/Shutterstock.com; p. 12 Mayskyphoto/Shutterstock.com; p. 13 Galyna Andrushko/Shutterstock.com; p. 14 Frederic Lewis/Staff/Archive Photos/Getty Images; pp. 15, 23 (Mount Rushmore) Nivek Neslo/Photodisc/Getty Images; p. 16 catwalker/Shutterstock.com; pp. 17, 22, 23 (Uncle Sam) UltraViolet/Shutterstock.com; pp. 18, 23 (statue) © iStockphoto.com/gregobagel; p. 19 Matej Hudovernik/Shutterstock.com; pp. 20, 22(Statue of Liberty) stockpix4u/Shutterstock.com; p. 21 Gavin Gough/Lonely Planet Images/Getty Images.

ISBN: 978-1-4488-8980-8
6-pack ISBN: 978-1-4488-8981-5

Manufactured in the United States of America

CPSIA Compliance Information: Batch #WS12RC: For further information contact Rosen Publishing, New York, New York at 1-800-237-9932.

Word Count: 180

Contents

What Is a Symbol? 4

Our Flag 6

The White House 8

Monuments 10

Mount Rushmore 13

Uncle Sam 16

Statue of Liberty 18

Symbols of the United States 22

Words to Know 23

Index 24

The United States has many symbols.
They teach us about our country.

A symbol is something
that stands for something else.

The United States has a flag.
It's red, white, and blue.

The flag has stars and stripes.

We see our flag in the sky.

Another symbol is the White House.

It's very big.

The White House is where the president leads the country.

Sometimes, a symbol can be a monument.

A monument is a building.

It honors something from our past.

The Washington Monument honors our first president, George Washington.

Mount Rushmore is another symbol.

The mountain has four faces on it.
The faces show some presidents.

Lots of people like to visit
Mount Rushmore.

Another symbol is Uncle Sam.

He tells us to love America.

Uncle Sam is old.

He has a white beard.

Our country has some symbols that are statues.

Statues can look like people or animals.

One symbol is the Statue of Liberty.

Liberty means that you are free to do things that others can't.

The Statue of Liberty tells people that Americans are free.

Symbols of the United States

Flag

Statue of Liberty

Washington Monument

Uncle Sam

White House

Words to Know

beard

flag

monument

mountain

statue

Index

flag, 6, 7, 22
free, 20, 21
liberty, 20
monument, 10, 11, 12
mountain, 14
Mount Rushmore, 13, 15
president(s), 9, 12
statue(s), 18, 19
Statue of Liberty, 19, 21, 22
Uncle Sam, 16, 17, 22
Washington Monument, 12, 22
White House, 8, 9, 22